FROM **IDEA** TO **BOOK**

by Pam Marshall

Lerner Publications Company / Minneapolis

The publisher would like to thank Nancy Carlson for her participation.

Copyright © 2004 by Lerner Publishing Group, Inc.

All rights reserved. International copyright secured. No part of this book may be reproduced, stored in a retrieval system, or transmitted in any form or by any means—electronic, mechanical, photocopying, recording, or otherwise—without the prior written permission of Lerner Publishing Group, Inc., except for the inclusion of brief quotations in an acknowledged review.

Lerner Publications Company
A division of Lerner Publishing Group, Inc.
241 First Avenue North
Minneapolis, MN 55401 U.S.A.

Website address: www.lernerbooks.com

Library of Congress Cataloging-in-Publication Data

Marshall, Pam.
   From idea to book / by Pam Marshall ; photographs by Todd Strand.
     p. cm. — (Start to finish)
   Includes index.
   Summary: Explains the process of making a book by following the production of Nancy Carlson's book, "It's Not My Fault!," through its stages of writing, illustrating, editing, designing, printing, and binding.
     ISBN-13: 978–0–8225–1385–8 (lib. bdg. : alk. paper)
     ISBN-10: 0–8225–1385–4 (lib. bdg. : alk. paper)
   1. Books—Juvenile literature. 2. Book industries and trade—Juvenile literature. [1. Books. 2. Book industries and trade.] I. Strand, Todd, ill. II. Title. III. Series: Start to finish (Minneapolis, Minn.)
   Z116.A2M36 2004
   002—dc22   2003020983

Manufactured in the United States of America
4 5 6 7 8 9 – DP – 13 12 11 10 09 08

The photographs in this book appear courtesy of Todd Strand/Independent Picture Service.

Table of Contents

The writer has an idea....4

The story is written......6

The story is sent to a publishing company.....8

The pictures are sketched..10

The art is finished......12

Computer files are made..14

The pages are printed....16

The paper is folded.....18

The cover is glued on....20

The book is ready to read..22

Glossary................24

Index.................24

It's fun to read picture books.
Let's see how they are made.

The writer has an idea.

Books start with an idea for a story. Sometimes the story is made up. Sometimes the story comes from real life. This writer has an idea for a picture book.

The story is written.

The writer finds the right words to tell the story. Her words make the story interesting, easy to understand, and fun.

The story is sent to a publishing company.

Publishing companies make books. The company decides which stories it wants to make into books. Those stories go to editors. An editor helps the writer improve the story.

The pictures are sketched.

This writer also draws the pictures for her books. First, she makes simple drawings called **sketches.** She shows her sketches to the designer at the publishing company. The designer makes sure the pictures will look nice in the book.

The art is finished.

The words and the sketches are just right. It is time to finish the art. Finished art goes into the book. The writer takes her time to make her pictures beautiful. She uses special markers and colored pencils.

13

Computer files are made.

Workers type the words into the computer. A special machine puts the art into the computer. The writer's pictures and words are in computer files. The editor and the designer make sure there are no mistakes in the files.

The pages are printed.

Printing plates are made from the computer files. Printing plates are like stamps. The plates go into a **printing press.** They are covered in ink. Many big sheets of paper also go through the printing press. Rollers press ink onto the paper. Some sheets are for inside the book. Here comes the outside of the book.

The paper is folded.

The inked paper is sent to the **bindery.** The bindery's machines fold the paper. The folded sheets become the book's pages. The machine stacks and sews groups of pages together. Then a machine trims the edges of the pages.

The cover is glued on.

Pages that show the book's name are glued onto pieces of cardboard. This makes the book's cover. Then the cover is glued onto the rest of the book.

The book is ready to read.

Trucks carry the books to stores and libraries. You can buy the book from the bookstore. You can check it out at the library. What's your favorite book?